TANK the T-REX

LEARNS HOW TO TELL THE TRUTH

written by Lucas Wurtz

illustrated by Maria Koallas

ISBN: 979-8-9855545-5-7

TANK the T-REX

LEARNS HOW TO TELL THE TRUTH

written by Lucas Wurtz
illustrated by Maria Koallas

Find us on Facebook

ShockOwl

THIS BOOK BELONGS TO ____________

"Hello Boys and Girls!

Let me introduce myself!

I'm Tank the T-Rex!

Do you know what I love more than anything in the whole world!?

Popsicles!!!!

Give me a high five if you
love popsicles too!

Wow! You are really good at high fives!

Give me one more!

Do you want to taste my popsicle?
I don't mind, but you better ask an
adult first.

This is the best day of my life!"

Burrrrpppppp

"Tank, did you eat <u>**ALL**</u> the popsicles?"

"Um no... Why do you ask, Dad?"

"There was a box of popsicles in the freezer.
Where did they all go?
Did you eat them?"

"No it wasn't me, Dad.
It must have been someone else."

"Are you sure you didn't eat them?"

"Yes, I'm sure."

“Tank, you wouldn’t lie,
would you?

You know that lying is bad and
that it’s always better to
tell the truth.”

"Nope, it wasn't me."

"Ok, I guess I'll have to tell the neighbors that the popsicles, for the party this weekend, are all gone."

"Oh no, I told a lie to my dad.
I did eat all the popsicles.

Do you think I should tell my dad the truth?

Hey Dad, I did eat all the popsicles.

I feel really bad. I didn't mean to eat them all. I didn't know you were going to share them with the neighbors.

I really like popsicles and
got carried away eating them.
I just thought they were so yummy."

“I’m glad you were honest and told me the truth. Lying is wrong and it will often lead to more trouble.

Let's go to the store and buy new popsicles to share with everyone."

“Wow, we sure learned an important lesson today didn’t we kids?

It's never good to tell a lie.
Always tell the truth!

I think some high fives are in order!

High five!

To the side!

To the other side!

Way down low!

Woah! Too Slow!

Thanks for reading with me today!

I'm going to buy some more yummy popsicles!"

Bonus Coloring Page

Thank you for reading
"TANK the T-REX
LEARNS HOW TO TELL THE TRUTH"

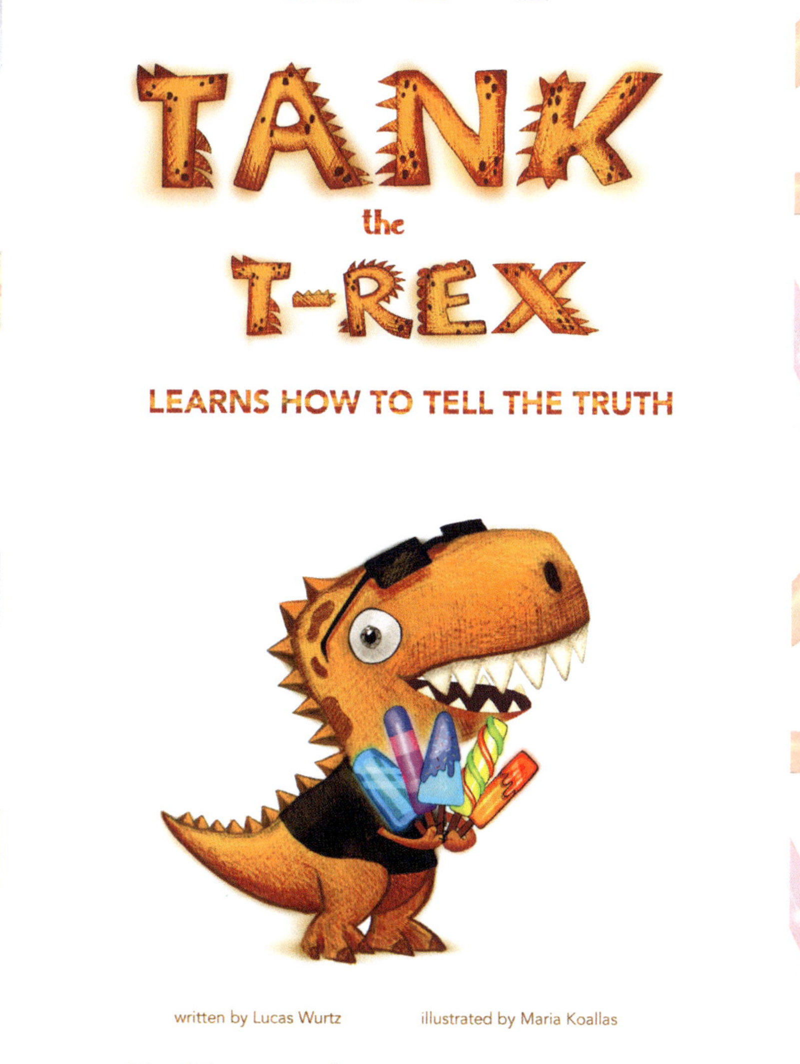

Enjoyed this book? Please leave a review!

Printed in Great Britain
by Amazon

38668660R00030